...Until We
See WONDERS

To Vantas,
from the defuncked
cotlette

. . . Until We See WONDERS

A Collection of Writing

Stella Rossellini

To order additional copies of this book, contact:
Xlibris LLC
0-800-056-3182
www.xlibrispublishing.co.uk
Orders@xlibrispublishing.co.uk
616595

CONTENTS

This collection of Poetry and Writing is wholeheartedly dedicated to the person dearest and closest, my mother and friend, who passed away suddenly in the beginning of this year.

The Silhouette

A young girl awoke, one night, to the sight of a tall dark creature, standing over her little bed. A dark silhouette which stood completely and utterly still. They glared at each other, silence piercing the little girls ears. The wind brushing her golden locks. The silhouette bent over carefully and asked the girl

"why does such young a beauty lay in this here bed? It is time, dearest. It is time to walk with me."

The girl simply starred at it with her deeply innocent and tearful crystal eyes. Her lashes long, they blinked away . . .

"why me?" she cried out.

"your brother is here with me." He replied.

"No! for my brother is long dead!"

"That is precisely why he's here beside me . . ." The silhouette bellowed.

There came a light beneath her door, the handle screeched. The girl swung her head with her hair draping over her eyes. She gasped, for the door was locked, yet opened wide before her. The ray of light blinded the girls frail blue eyes. A figure moved slowly out from the light towards her. The girl then sighed, "Peter."

"Yes, he's here, as you see, he wants you to come home with him . . ." Said the silhouette . . .

"Mommy's waiting . . ." Peter declared to the little sister.

The little sister then cried to this, out of breath. "No Peter, No! Mommy can't be waiting!"

"Oh, but she is. She has been for a very long time now."

"I miss mommy . . . ." Sobbed the girl in remorse.

"Then 'tis time" Said the shadow.

A diamond tear rolled down her pink cheek, it sparkled all the way down to her cold little hands. She then took the covers off, placed her feet in her slippers and got up. Heading towards the light, the shadow en clothed her gently around the shoulders. So warm and calming it was, and in they went.

Then came the next morning, the little girls' nurse came round her room to wake her up, yet found her dead . . . Her skin white, the lips blue and the eyes closed. The wind still brushing through her hair. The sun shimmering outside her window, and the nurse shouted for help while the birds sang a song of bliss.

Ode to a Funny Little Man

A funny little man said to me,
He once lived by the sea.
Darling, I, from Argentine,
Have stories that are mine,
Yes darling, of great a many lovers!
And here now, his story uncovers.
Hahaha and hehehe
For I am just a man!
With dark hair and a tan.
There is no shame in that.
I let them think that I'm a mat,
For if I did not
My story would rot.
Oh hahaha and hehehe!
He stares at me and waits,
Before he tells the story of his mates.
Why yes darling, of course!
Warhol too was quite on course!
But when he glanced at me,
It gave me less than glee.
Yet all the while still, to me he came.
You might say, I was found by fame,
Timeless treasures I did receive,
Yet 'twas time for me to leave.
Ahahaha darling.
On one occasion he brought to me,
Lord of fashion, from what I see.
"This is Gianni, Gianni will look after you."
Now this one too, was quite on cue.
He covered me in dresses fine,
And let me know that all was mine.
By now I felt supreme,
Which was now a common theme.
Yet one day soon,
From out the blue moon,
I heard Andy was no more,

And no one told me all the gore.
A decade rolled on by,
'twas time for another fair good bye.
Oh my darling dear,
A mansion he opened not so near.
It was celebrated well,
Yet to me he did not tell.
Until later some news came,
Of a man who was to blame.
Three shots Gianni, three shots,
Bang bang bang, it echoed lots.
Hehehe oh hahaha,
And so I listened closer still,
Of this man's strong, wild will.
As he began again to say,
That later come another day.
I rollered down the park,
With legs so long and dark.
An Irish ladie then cried out
All and ready with a pout,
Yes darling, haha!
I turned and flipped the bird,
For a second no sound was heard,
"You're from Puerto Rico, are you not?"
No I am of the Argentine lot!
"Oh dear, oh dear for I am of the Irish gold"
Ireland, a land I was never ever told!
All the gold he would later give,
14 years together did we live.
Then later still there came a day,
When tragedy came out to play.
The twins that stood so high,
Were no longer seen by the eye,
And so that day would start an age,
All new and on a page.
And so my Irish dear,
Lost his ways to fear,
Friends he lived for,
Were gone forever more.

Indeed then came another day
I would venture far away,
And here I sit today!
Reminiscing, in a way
Oh darling! That is my life!
Destiny, his true wife,
And so I sit,
And laugh a bit.
The funny little man danced away,
So human, he did say,
That, so true,
Is far from new.
For he was but a man,
And pleasures he did not ban.
Indeed this was his code,
Though God is of a different mode,
For God, he loves us still,
For we are far from nil,
All those a little queer,
Love is truly clear.

'Tis but a cold dark morning;
As my eyes gaze out into the distance . . .
Once, the days not long ago-
Sang to me
And my life sprang with joy.
As though it were constant spring.
I knew no other life then.
The life of pure and natural beauty.
Oh how it spoke to me, and how it sang!
In the distant ocean I saw promises galore,
Promises which God fulfils.
Out there in the far horizon,
Where the sun meets the sea,
Looking out my window, now,
I dream the day I reach-

Perfection, Peace . . .
The love of God so great,
So unconditional . . .
Oh now I anticipate his love
And yet, 'tis still a cold dark morning . . .
Although tomorrow, the sun shall rise again,
It will shine greater than ever before.
I shall bask in the love of God yet again.
My eyes will glow with life that shall return to me once more.

The Twist of Saturn

Your life remains unfinished,
Come, come over here I said.
Settle, settle here . . .
And he says to me, But I've been wondering sleepless nights.
Then I said onto him, have you ever held Saturn in your hand? Has it ever
spun round and round and round?
No, he answered, but a star blinded my eyes so it stung my heart . . .
Hush, I says to him. Do you feel the aggravated heat of Mercury? I think if
comes for you.
Nah, Mercury would have nothing to do with me. Ah, but don't be so hasty,
now! I said to him, it will creep up on everyone sooner or later. You just . . .
have to . . . let him in.
And then the clouds rolled on by with furious anguish.
They left without a trace.
I think someone wants to speak to you.
And who would that be? He says to me.
I don't know . . . look . . . why don't you go and . . . ask.
Suddenly then with a slight breeze, those gates of gold opened tenderly as a
page turned by the wind.
Gushing mist flowed out of them.
And so he marched, heart of iron, mind of steel and love on his lips.
I stared in awe as the gates closed steadily behind him, leaving me in
waiting . . .
For the star with piercing gaze.
The land is vast. It spins complete.
Diamonds then gushed out from the sky,
As the children played.

A Lonely Room

A room full of prized possessions,
Is no room at all
Where is the love?
There is nothing but death here . . .
Collecting dust . . .
With its foul stench in the air.
In every breeze.
It lurks around and crawls deep.
Deep beneath the skin.
Oh where is the love, I say?!
 I come to fight this desolation.
Through the thickness of the dust,
I break through the unbeatable.

Away

I look around, but see no eyes.
There are no stars here.
Only buzzards picking at my feet.
Time for a holiday!
But only sometimes,
Sometimes, the leopard brings me chains and shackles in the middle of the
night.
So I sit by the cold and silent lake,
I stare at him.
Wondering when oh when, this battle will be won?
So I come out of hiding, with stallions at my side.
They carry me back, back to Africa
And return me to my wild freedom.
Welcome! They exclaim
Clothing me in warm rain
Drenching me in passion.

Emperor

They stare at me, but once,
Not twice.
They won't tell me where he's buried . . .
But the Emperor sits high and mighty in his place,
	Watching over all . . .
The walls speak, they hold no rumours,
But as I run round and round,
The Emperor still watches,
I realise this is where they assemble,
	Delivering bodies to his feet.
This is the land where cannibals reign.
Wicked is this land of running blood.
And the Emperor still stares from his mighty place,
	Without a blink . . .
And I too, feel no more,
	As my eyes remain fixed forever more.

Take a deep breath, now
Yes, and make no vow.
For freedom is not hard to master,
But if you blink faster,
I dare say he'll turn,
Just to fall and burn.
Afraid of Holy majesty.
Our love is but a travesty.
For what we have is but a farce.
And Grace is all and sparse.
It lands not at your feet,
But gives an earthly heat.
Devine is Grace,
With faithful pace.
All in all, it loves you dear,
And drives off all your fear.

Generation

Sounds of a dead generation.
And how long will you sleep?
Has the work been done,
      All for you?
A thick glass that lends no ear.
Smart you are not, dead you are.
A whisk of techno transferring you.
Fibre. Glass. Fibre glass . . .
The heart of a dead generation.
Vast green oceans
Drip drip from thy ear.
On top of your ant hill,
Drenching it with fibre glass of green.
The soil rotten now, it will lash out.
It whispers not, but screams out loud.
Crude and deadly with precision,
This generation of ours,
It glides into a future
That holds it not

Legend

Oh dearest children of thy lands,
Come hither, lend your ears!
For a notion must be heard.
I've come far and travelled wide,
Though never have I heard such fun . . .
They call you . . . Legendary.
Are you a LEGEND, child?
Dost' thou speak?
Or dost' thou listen?
Legends . . .
'Tis the stuff dreams are made of.
Fable and heroic, ancient and so traditional.
I ask you again child!
Are thou ancient? Hast thou lived the times and bore all witness?
Dost' thou call himself a hero?
I ask you this,
Are thou immortal?
Or hast' thou actions proven immortality?
Know now, time stands by my side, infinitely . . .
Know now, only time knows who you are.
Time, meddles with thy heart, for it collects all witness.
Take good care,
All, children of mine.
And know this notion now,
For value so easily slips,
If no care is there.

The Serpent Slayer

There once came a man,
Of joy and salvation he sang!
Teach me master,
Teach me hope.
Preach to me of Holy Paradise!
And so he did,
  As was promised.
Here, he arrived to save the day.
The day for all ages.
Our one true knight.
Though dresses in armour he was not,
Clothed in destiny he was.
He slayed the devilish serpent
And brought back what was ours.

The Scene

This is the scene, man . . .
Come and join,
For this is the scene.
Lines are blurred,
For the scene is here.
Make a choice,
Join the scene

The I, in Idiot

I was born of thee,
And run so gay and free!
I don't know what they want from me,
When I look onto the sea,
Somehow all I want is tea!
When I run in undies gay and free,
I often need to wee,
But they keep staring right at me,
I still don't know what they want from me!
So I lean against a tree,
And let out all of me!
For I don't care if they flee . . .
Yes, Hi! My name is Lee!
For I let myself be,
So gay and free.
And for you on one knee,
I laugh with glee.
Please, do marry me!
For I run gay and free.

Walking Over My Grave

On one spring night,
I walked into the marsh,
And there I heard a voice.
  The wind spoke and told me
  "Now stop."
Then I looked down . . .
And here, my body would lie.
For then I knew my resting place.
By the foxes here,
  And all my other friends.
So I lay down my ear
And listened to the heart beat
  Of old' sweet mother of mine.
Shhh . . .
Silence now . . . she speaks . . .
The stars, they shimmered quite.
Now one day,
They will gather and they will sing,
  To bring me back . . .
A soul so long departed.
Oh yes, they will speak to me!
But the crickets chirped
And the night stayed put.
Yet all the while,
Footsteps shuffled past this site . . .
So there I laid a while more,
  In all this lace galore.
My good old friend, the owl,
He sat there still
  With eyes blazing.
And all my fairy friends,
Gently sang in angelical choirs.
Until the great old sun arose and said
  "Awake. You go home now."
So then I went to count my days,
But I hear them clapping
A sweet sweet serenade.

The Weeping Gallows

And one summer morning you awoke . . .
And screamed . . .
And cried . . .
And dared not speak its name.
The weeping gallows called,
      With filth and pride.
Oh joy to lonely nights.
Although your ancestors whisper in your ear
      Love, Love, love . . . love . . .
So far, yet so near.
All those days forgotten
They drown the morning still,
      In savage waste.

Thee Above

Life is but a journey-
A journey of lustrous gold.
Divinity in thou eyes.
Glory in thou heart.
Of honesty I speak to thee
Thee, so high above
For thee speaks but honestly to me.
I know not of love,
More greater and divine
Than sincerity of the world
Than thee above

Hey Mama

Hey there, mama,
Don't you cry for me.
Hey dear mama,
Oh let me be.
For dawn is near
And surely I will sing,
      Sweet melody's to you.
Oh mama, just let me be.
I hold you near,
      Oh so near.
But you gotta let me go,
      Now, mama . . .
No dreams will spill,
Oh no heart will crumble.
Yes, dear mama
For I have you,
      Right beside me.

Queen of Game

Eyes of amber,
Fur of gold.
Heart of steel,
Love of passion,
This breed so pure.
Majesty, nobility.
Oh, Queen of Egypt,
Lay yourself in peace,
Oh Daisy, dear.
The Afghan hunting Queen.

The Press

Repress,
Suggest,
Repress the rest.
The rest digress.
Digress the rest,
The rest is less,
And less repress.
Suggest . . .

And in the midst of darkness,
There appears a light.
For it is warm, it is Holy.
It nurtures fully . . .
Hold onto the light.
It creates miracles,
For they too happen,
All full of heart.

Living atrocities stay close,
Oh, what do you want with us?
Yet together we remain,
And here we stand.
United, under earthly blankets.
You scare us not,
For we remain stronger still,
Standing here . . .
As cold as it may be,
You will strip us not of life,
For we live until the day is won to freedom.

The Night

Forgive the day
And learn the night.
Stand close,
      But do not stir . . .
Learn its wisdom,
Learn its cause.
Soothingly it speaks,
      For silently it loves.
Ask it questions,
It will smile . . .
The night holds secrets, oh so fine
For lives are offered,
      On this dream boat of chance.

Regret no more

Regret nothing.
Cry for nothing.
Your soul is forever endless.
    For it is sufficient.
Pain may come,
    Pain may go.
For the soul lives past the now
    It speaks to the universe.
Yet Mars will point otherwise
    He stands gallant and rigid
Control and power he has not,
    He may look past . . .
    He stares deep.
    Elegant and strong.
Body withers . . .
Yet the soul remains unbreakable
Whether truth be bearable
    Or not . . .
The soul will sing,
    And sing it will.
For good and evermore.

Angel of Lust

Breeze blew past my chest.
I took a deep breath, and smiled . . .
    With happiness . . .
    Whole hearted happiness,
For when I opened my eyes, and stretched my arms,
You were there-beside me.
Like the morning rose, a young bud . . .
    Like a fresh dewy bottle of milk,
    Every morning,
    Of every day . . .
A ray of walking sunshine you are!
    My button eyes . . . .
You left that morning,
    As you regularly do . . . .
And I sigh
    Waiting-
To see those dewy button eyes once more.

That night,
As any other night . . .
I walk down the burning streets of pleasure.
With sounds,
    Amplifying from every door.
So this here, is my life-
    Gasps and moans, pleads and sighs.
My body burns
Yet no sign of my button eyed angel.
Though I blink a few times,
Red, red, red lights zap into my frail eyes
    Oh I'm tired . . .
I walk to where I know not
    Eyes blink, eyes flash
    Bodies moulding, bodies sweating
And there I stop . . .
Music pumping blood.
Neon's flickering,

Lips pouting,
Heart thumping
Advertisement screams evil!
Hold me . . .
  Hold me tender,
No sign of the button eyed angel.
Heart races, mouth on fire
Lips dance
  They melt like cream.
But only I exist.
  Only I live
Hands slipping easily down,
  Body on fire
  Vacuum . . .
When eyes are closed,
  At the end of the hopeless tunnel of unknown darkness,
I see those button eyes of brown.
But the days repeat themselves.
  In closed agony of addiction.

And so the next morning,
I take a deep breath and sigh and smile,
  Of whole hearted happiness,
I saw my button eyes of brown,
  For he kissed me dear,
  And stroked me fine.
And that night-
As any other night,
The streets burned as they do every day.
Like the sun they glow.
  They flinch.
Some survived, others didn't.
  But are replaced by new lights,
And so they appear.
  One after the other,
In endless cosmos of design.
As I then again felt the passionate hands of lust upon me
  Until I saw my button angel eyes once more.

Forget me not

Corpses rotting,
Angels singing,
Cannon balls crashing,
Flowers blooming,
Children screaming,
The world illuminated . . .
Nightmares become dreams,
      Dreams become nightmares . . .

Hello mother for I am dead,
Hello father for I am dead.
You see me not,
      Though cry no more.
I was good to you,
      And you loved me too.
Hold me tight, mamma,
      Don't let go.

We demolish this time that is no more . . .

Yet somehow,
Love/life finds a way . . . .

Hear them marching,
Hear them jumping.
Walk past me not!
Scream to me!

They do as they please.

And so here, I say,
        I loved you, dear.
For land is young,
        But fire is old.
Forgive me, dear,
For they got me first.

Good night sweet corpses,
And let those birdies sing to you.
        Goodnight, goodnight
        Farewell, farewell.

Colourful Emptiness

This world of ours,
A colourful place, indeed . . .
Never fully understood,
Unidentifiable . . .
For knowledge is infinite
Yet life is finite.
Just when you think you've come to know something-
It changes its form,
Illusive, transparent.
This here world of ours contains
A multitude of colours and spectrums.
It changes shape, dimensions . . .
They fold in, fold out.
It breathes.
Sings songs to us,
Puts us to sleep,
It tells us stories-
Of ancient wonders and splendorous masks.
This world never stays still,
For it evolves.
And yet . . .
History repeats itself,
A colourful world of emptiness-

Yet nothing ever happens . . .

Lies Speak

Boldly, lies speak.
Speak painfully,
Speak truthfully,
    O' rose budded lips . . .
Please, do listen to thy heart,
    And hurt me not
    With words of rust.
Separate thyself not,
    From thou mind, thou heart.
For thou art one.
    One in a million,
One who lies so sweet,
One with gift of lust.
The book of lies-
    Bestowed upon thy head,
Engraved directly, on thou rose budded lips.
Yet, yonder high, an angel awaits ye,
    Oh yea, he doth.
O' dearest rose budded lips,
    Disappoint him not.

A Wound in Salt

See how the tears stream,
The pain, untameable.
     Numb to affection.
And oh how the body is an open wound,
     A living corpse!
It lies beneath a salted shower detest.
And oh how the daggers hit upon either temple!
See how the body is chained . . .
Days and months slip,
     And the salt keeps dripping . . .
My mother still sits beside me,
     Weeping . . .
I see you Mother!
     Wont you rescue me?
But she kept on weeping.
So the moon took whole,
And cast me into darkness.
It left me-
     All alone in the night.
By now, mother drifted away,
But there I lay shackled in despair.
     Frail and human,
     Cold and bleeding.

There sits, me thinks a man,
A little old man.
Gazing into a puddle,
The little old man,
He seems but far from gregarious,
The little old man.
For sitting there, the snow, it would appear,
To be gleefully landing upon his big dry nose,
The little old man.
For his eyes were as dead as night,
As unloving and unthinking as the dead.
For there he sat, and sat some more.
Until the breath would come no more.
The little old man.

Man is born

Man Lives!
For man is born . . . alas man dies.
'Tis the sacred ritual
They say you come as one,
     You leave as one.
Man sins!
Man is Holy . . .
But man, is nothing but a creature.
He is . . . a complex creation of God
Though still,
He is of a mammal . . .
     He is-animal
He is a creature . . .
For he was designed so . . .
In the beginning,
     There was-
In the beginning-God.
Though he is just that-
     The beginning . . .
Or rather, the ONLY beginning.
Lets just say . . . a term simpler,
Though perhaps more complicated by definition,
     Than GOD . . .
"in the *beginning* God created . . ."—Genesis 1:1
Term beginning, stands before
     The term God, it stands stronger.
Therefore . . .
Infinity, or beginning stands unknown to the naked eye of man.
Man stands of flesh . . .
He is but a part of the living cycle.
The cycle of flesh
Man, cannot use all of the brain matter provided.
     Man was given senses . . .
     Five . . .
     Physical-of the flesh,
     For he was designed so . . .

Man was given choice . . .
    According to his design.
To be created in the likeness of God.
God bears the only witness.
God is the only truth,
    For he is the witness.
He is the beginning-and the end
Alpha and omega.
Though man has accessed "knowledge"
    Man has been given "truth"
Though man is but simply a creation of the flesh
    The ultimate design.
Man, cannot see infinity with his naked eye . . .
    For man is finite . . .
    Man is complex . . .
Man is not God,
    Nor will he ever be.
    Man is tricky . . . . .
Man is mightier than the beast, lower than the heavens . . .
    He is forever trapped in his quest for infinity
Man is but physical . . .
He feeds and learns off what has been provided.
    Man adapts . . .
    Man is tameable . . .
    Man is breakable
    Man is . . . subjective . . .
    For man perceives . . .
    He is of the flesh.
Man does not use all brain matter
Man is but a creature
He is full of fear . . .
    He fears that-what cannot be explained or understood
Therefore, perception remains,
    Experience stays.
    Man is tameable,
    Man is subjective . . .
Therefore, man will not know
The truth that is God-
    Man will never see, the beginning . . .

For man bears no witness . . .
For he is of the flesh
For man is a creation of the universe
    Man learns . . .
Man does not know-ALL
Man is finite
Man . . . is but a LIKENESS of God
    Man is not God
    Nor will he ever be . . .
Man is but a creature
    That learns and perceives
Man is of the flesh
Man is a servant
    A complex servant,
    That knows no better . . .
Man is born alone, he dies alone.
For that is how God invented him

"And if God did not exist, it would be necessary to invent him" . . .

                                      -Voltaire

                Fierce and luminous,
               The furs she shall wear.
        Delicate is her stream of passion.
      As she steadily gazes at herself,
           At the wonder that is,
   The beauty that was bestowed upon her.
             For she thinks,
             Is undying . . .
       But gaze you will, in her eyes,
          She dances no more.

I swam a distant sea,
A sea of wondrous delight.
For it held wisdom galore.
A deceitful vision,
A vision of distrust.
Corruption all around.
The waves have lost all harmony.
Enraged they are,
Beating themselves savagely against the rugged shores of hell,
Although hell would frown upon us.
For no sun nor moon can save us now.
Help us here,
Help us now
For salvation is all around,
But away from us, it is . . . .
Mystical as the Bible,
The Help left us stranded behind.

I see the burning eyes
I loathe the raging cries
I hear the yonder skies
Until the friendly thunder flies

What is your love worth?
Why trouble the future,
With what is so clear?
Would you really want to wreck the skies with fury?
Saviour, you are not.
Healer, you are not.
Away with your brutality and let come what may.

Why does your mother weep?
Weep for what may come?
Perhaps 'tis all nothing but an illusion.
Illusion filled with lives,
Immortality and ongoing fusion.
The truth will point to itself.
It does not meddle with falsehood.

This is the era of great pride.
The pride of a wonderer.
The wondering soul that is no more
No more existence,
But this is the pain of evermore.
For pain brings salvation galore.
It is on a highway of tears.
A journey of ongoing fears.
Fears which enchant the mind.
The greatest treasures you'll ever find . . .

Do the dead truly watch?
Do the dead truly see?
A child that stands alone,
Will stand against the shattering clouds.
I watch you, my child.
For you will truly reign.

There hangs a mirror on the wall
Before it stands a woman in a shawl.
All was silent around,
For no being was ever found.
She lived, but never alone.
The voices come and moan,
The sun hangs upside down
Causing the moon to frown,
For the woman was of one,
Of darkened moon and shinning sun
She slithered in the day
Letting beings be her prey
Yet the mirror oh so silent,
But the noises grew ever violent.
This house disturbed us more and more.
Penetrating deeply to the core.
Our souls would cry of fear,
She ripped our deepest tear.
For the voices grew so ever near.

Darkness upon us . . .
Era of eternal night
Can words possibly describe the storm that has come?
Are words strong enough to warn, to rescue?
For greed has entered in.
It's been welcomed . . .
It penetrated every soul,
Turning bodies rotten.

49

A spectacle of lost hope.
The eyes of a woman.
So full of innocent life.
Her heart beats passionately,
Thumping and pounding
Through her chest.
She looks up to her beloved idol.
He shown a ray of eternal happiness and bliss onto her.
She was clean still . . .
She was nervous still . . .
Yet alone in the night she sat, patiently waiting for her beloved idol.
The man of heavenly spirit and high ideal.
He would cast her into darkness, one day.
Leaving her behind.
A tyrant he turned out to be
Of unholy being he was,
Which possessed a hungry wretched soul.
Fowl and haunting,
For this idol deceived the little one,
And left behind an embittered legacy of unearthly pleasure.
To haunt and cause the girl great and eternal pain.
And still she sits and awaits her "beloved idol"
Which would never return
To her arms . . .
To her bosom . . .
For appreciating the heart is a complicated task
For some to manage . . .

One mustn't be judged,
For he will be judged himself.
You see thee?
Standing on thy knees
Praying and praying.
Thy clock is ticking,
But wait!

There is still time . . .
For time is infinite,
'Tis the white shinning light,
Hope shall always be present,
Of life you shall think and live on.

Time and time again,
We venture into insanity.
Flowing in, flowing out.
Sliding in, oozing down.
Overfilling our life.
It falls apart.

Remorseful Beach

I glanced into the distant ocean,
  And saw nothing but strange devotion.
Covered in clouds and mist,
  My heart ached and twist.
A story I did not foresee,
  It refused to set me free.
Closer, there came a ghost,
  Of one I loved the most.
Red, were the skies,
  With furry of human ties.
I trudge along the beach,
  Reality aside and out of reach.
And the ghost still followed me along,
  To spread the secrets of my wrong.
Wind crept up my neck,
  A girl who turned a wreck.
I cried for the girl I once knew,
  Her heart was young and true.
So eagerly, she ran,
  Towards the heart of man.
Yet collapsed in a net,
  Regretting they ever met.
A whirlwind of fears,
  And cries of loathsome tears.
The calm evening sky,
  Soothes my droning cry.
The girl who was once me,
  Is now cold yet free.

Lithuanian Version

As zvilgtelejau i tolima vandenyna,
ir nieko nepamaciau tik keista atsidavima.
Paskendus debesyse ir ruke
mano sirdis sopejo ir virpejo.
Pasaka, kurios negalejau numatyti
atsisake islaisvinti mane.
Arciau priejo vele,
to, kuri mylejau labiausiai.
Raudoni buvo dangus,
zmoniu rysiu neapykanta.
As slinkau pajuriu,
realybe sone ir nepasiekiama.
Vele seka mane visalaik,
isduot mano blogio paslaptis.
Vejas priselino prie mano kaklo,
mergina liko sugniuzdyta.
As verkiau del merginos, kuria kazkada pazinojau,
jos sirdis buvo jauna ir tikra.
Nekantriai ji bego
link vyro sirdies.
Ji pargriuvo tinkle,
gailedamasi sutikus ji.
Baimiu ir neapykantos asaru sukurys.
Raminantis vakaro dangus
numalsina mano rauda.
Mergina, kuria kazkada buvau,
dabar salta bet laisva.

Loneliness spreading,
Covering from head to toe.
Having no mercy,
        No sense of time.
Letting you deal with it yourself.
Holding nothing back,
It reveals all of its power and might.
Loneliness spreading,
It's here to take control,
Knowing no peace
It barges into your very world
        Unwanted
        Uncalled for
        Like a disease . . .
Never retreating
For trudges forward,
On and on and on.

                        The Piercing cat eyes,
                    Glare out into the distant sky,
                Looking through a stainless window,
                        He sits breathlessly,
                        Waiting for answers . . .
                Warm tears roll down his velvety cheek.
                        They shimmer and glisten.
                        Sitting obediently,
                        He sighs . . .
                He no longer has time to purr.
            At times he shivers from the cool breeze.
                        His eyes still stare,
                    Reflecting the wise moon.
                        His heart pounding,
                    Only that could be heard,
                In the midst of the old night.

55

The minutes and hours stop,
But it keeps on beating . . .
The tears keep on rolling.
The crave for passion burns.
Alone,
He sits in silence,
Reality dissolving,
He catches his amber eyes closing,
He sighs once more . . .

Dazing at you fool,
Sitting here, I weep.
Weeping, I sit.
Thinking of you,
    For better days . . .
I hope and do believe,
But my mind cannot comprehend,
The daring moves I do take,
    Appearing to be absurd.
    Rather, irrelevant . . .
Unaccepted and condemned
And so here I weep,

      Of all the beautiful things,
      You must've seen
      You haven't seen the world . . .
      Life in itself.
      The bliss the times,
      The joy, the strength.
      While your tears flow,
      The sands of time twirl away.
      Along with them,
      Eyes sparkle,
      Yet all fake.
      Attempt of bliss parishes away
      And is lost for ages.
      Slumber casts upon
      The inner world
      Lights beaming down.
      The window sill.
      Are now fading into the distance.
      Off they go!
      And enter the world of darkness
      Once more . . .
      For yet another era
      Blindness . . .

Dare you say,
"I am the one."
When you gazed into,
The distant future,
You found a life of beauty,
You found a life of belief,
You found a life of trust,
And when you asked,
"will I be here?"
They roared a laugh!
A laugh so pure in confidence.
It smashed a brick wall.
You might have been shocked,
You did not hesitate to smile,
A smile of dry satisfaction.
A smile of a hissing snake.
You did not get your answer,
An answer you will never get
And so you'll live in deceit-
An imaginary shell,
That grows around you,
And so you'll sit in delusional wisdom,
Till they think it right.

When the music plays
We carry on dancing,
Try to deceive . . .
All you can,
Dance until you're dizzy,
Dance until you fall.
No one will see
And no one will know
You'll be there,
And there you'll stay.
Till seasons pass
For all eternity.

59

The Window in the Forehead

Deep in the jungle, nature speaks. [1]La selva Amazonica conversa con el viento. The leaves, they make such a fuss . . .

But just around the corner now, there dwells a man. He lives but by his mirror and tells it all. But on this dark occasion, [2]el espeja amable, revealed it true and what did the little man find? With enchanted horror he gazed at the window in his forehead.

[3]!Oh, Dios! He cried loud and clear. The branches out there, they keep rustling. He could touch it not, for the pain, it stung so queer. All was dark past the window, it did not bleed. The surgery complete. He slowly then lit a flame to reveal more. !Oh Dios! [4] El cerebro, que esta ahi! For it seemed it had a life of its own. As the light moved closer still, our friend could only see it quiver and breathe.

Oh day of days . . .

[5]!Rapido ahora, hay que escondio!

And so our hero, he tied it thrice, not twice, and ran into the distant valley. He climbed the lavish land and sang it songs and danced a dance.

'Twas not long before he reached his horses. Some were starved, some were crippled. All were lonely. They smelled of unjust death, they twitch not, for they must save their days. But as he moved on down, his friends, they somehow grew. He came upon the largest one and asked.

[6]?Hablar rapidamente, quien hizo esta ventana?

[7]Oh, pero por supuesto que usted quiere saber . . . ?Preferiria pedir a un culo o un aguila?

Not one second later did the giant creature rise and plunge itself down towards the "ass" and man. He might have been no phoenix, though its magic was just the same. Its wings as white as snow, they flapped a pulse. Boom . . . boom boom . . . boom boom. And as the phoenix, his legacy too

---

[1]   The Amazon rainforest converses with the wind

[2]   The friendly mirror

[3]   Oh lord/God

[4]   The brain, its there

[5]   Quickly now, it must be hid

[6]   Speak quickly, who made this window

[7]   Oh but of course you'd want to know, would you rather ask an ass or an eagle

it reigned. He cast no glance, and flew right past our hero and friends. It landed beside a tired old man, his beard a trail of tears.

[8]!Que era yo! Asi tiere que ser.

And the Horses chuckled amongst themselves . . .

[9]?No has aprendido? El espejo quiere llevarte. Y asi que me pare aqui.

Then the honourable eagle bestowed its glance at our dear ol' friend for he was shocked, but lived to breathe another day. Although, the storm it comes so soon. He shall be waiting by the distant seas that hit the land. They'll hit and hit some more, until the moon swallows the sun and days. Until he grows his own wings and flaps himself away. Flaps until he reaches his own master of a different land, not all that far away.

---

[8]   'Twas I, it must be so

[9]   Have you not learned? The mirror wants to take you away

17678905R00039

Printed in Great Britain
by Amazon